The Secret of Great Italian Cooking

Recipes and Reflections of a Love Shared through Food

Monica Haughey

Maria Grazia Furnari

D1394077

the good food initiative

connecting people to good food

www.goodfoodinitiative.ie

© 2015 Monica Haughey & Maria Grazia Furnari

Creative Assistance Clare Mathews

Pages iv and v, vix , xvi Francesco Ancona
Page vi Michelle O'Sullivan
Page xxii, 40 Hugh Mc Elveen
Pages xxvi, 3, 11 , 22, 33 , 37, 42   Lido Vannucchi

ISBNS
Parent : 978-1-78237-976-8
epub: 978-1-78237-977-5
mobi: 978-1-78237-978-2
PDF: 978-1-78237-979-9

A cip catalogue for this book is available from the National Library.

Published by Original Writing Ltd., Dublin, 2015.

Printed by Essentra, Glasnevin, Dublin 11

This book is dedicated to the Eagar and Furnari families

in Ireland and Italy

Acknowledgements

Thanks to Laura Lastrucci, Silvio Venturi, Naima Fornaci,

Lina Leanza and Lucia Leanza for assistance with photographs.

Thanks also to Fabio Pracchia for inspiring conversations on Italian Food

and Siobhan Bourke for editing and support.

Thanks to Mamma Ro' in Lucca.

Monica Haughey

Introduction

Monica Haughey

For many years my late sister-in-law, Paula Eagar, came back and forth from her new found home in Sicily laden with mouth watering gifts for her family in Ireland. She came with large chunks of Parmesan cheese, delicious local wine and large bottles of Olive oil, known to her family as "good" Olive oil.

She had had fallen in love with and married Aldo Furnari, a Sicilian, in 1968 whom she met while studying in Milan. She had fallen in love not only with Aldo, but also with Sicily and especially with Italian food and culture. Similarly, Paula's Irish family enjoyed traveling to Sicily and experiencing first hand a very different and romantic culture that they thrived on during their summer holidays.

Paula Eagar

When Paula came home to Ireland on holidays in the summer, her gifts of Italian food were highly prized and somewhat novel. The fresh Parmesan and large bottles of Olive oil weren't used in Ireland at that stage. Paula was introducing her Irish family to the pleasures and sensual delights of the Italian food culture in which she had become immersed. Her son Carmelo shocked Paula's parents but delighted their neighbours by knocking on doors in Dartmouth Square in Dublin asking to harvest their snails, as he wanted to make a pasta sauce.

For my wedding in Dublin, Paula managed to travel from Sicily with six beautiful pasta bowls and a very large and fragile serving bowl, once again, to somehow maintain the links between Italy, her home country of Ireland and the people she loved.

The strong connection between our Irish and Sicilian families have continued since Paula passed away in 2009. Since marrying into the Eagar family, I have enjoyed many trips to Sicily and visited Paula's daughters, Maria Grazia Furnari and Sara Furnari in Lucca and Milan. Holidays with the Furnari family involves much discussion about food and dining with large and ever-changing numbers of Italians. I have enjoyed eating lots of different pasta dishes, beautiful fresh fish and foraged wild mushrooms, asparagus and anything else in season.

In the summer of 2014, under the banner of *The Good Food Initiative*, Paula's daughter, Maria Grazia Furnari, led two cookery classes in my home in Dublin. Maria Grazia's classes were wonderful and inspirational even though all who attended were already well able to cook! This prompted me to think further about the links through food between our Irish family and Paula's Italian family.

I began to wonder what the "big deal" was about Italian cooking. Why did we all love so much the experience of watching and tasting the food she made? Why are we Irish so allured by Italian cooking and what was it that Maria Grazia's parents really brought home to Ireland with the Olive oil and cheese and other wholesome food?

Since Paula first traveled back from Sicily, Irish food culture has become richer and more diverse and we now enjoy a wider choice of ingredients. We have artisan producers making fantastic mozzarella, we have a multitude of other world class local cheeses and fresh produce in our farmers' markets. An increasing number of supermarkets supply fresh organic produce from home and abroad. When preparing for the cookery classes it came as a surprise to Maria Grazia that all of her ingredients were now available in Ireland and that she did not need, like her mother before her, to covertly stash them in a suitcase!

Yet it does seem that the Italians have something special to offer us around food. In this short book, Maria Grazia and I have taken some time to explore the connection between our two countries, through food and family. Maria Grazia has given us recipes that she herself loves and prepares every day and that she has inherited from her own family whilst growing up in Sicily. Others recipes she has learnt from her friends in the different regions of Emilia Romagna and Tuscany where she has lived. Her repertoire has also been enriched by those recipes she has created from her own intuitive sense and love of cooking.

Alongside the recipes, we explore what is behind our love of Italian cooking, what we can learn from it and how we can incorporate it into our own culture. Maria Grazia describes her appreciation of food and its centrality in our lives, not only in its role to nourish and satisfy but also in its wider meaning.

A Sicilian farmer
checking his oranges
are ripe for picking.

We can make daily choices that have an impact on our health and on the people we care about and on the health of the environment

Maria Grazia Furnari

My Italian Family Background

Maria Grazia Furnari

I was born in Sicily with Irish and Sicilian parents . My mum came from what was in many ways a traditional Irish family, but where education and travelling were priorities even at times when money was not plentiful.

My father came from Adrano, a big Sicilian farming town, made famous by a farmers' revolt in the 1950's to claim ownership of the land in what was at that time a quasi-feudal system. His father was a farmer who went into the countryside every day on his donkey to bring home fresh fruit and vegetables. His sister, (Graziella) the woman I took my first name from, had a *salumeria* (grocery) on the main square where, even in post war times, you would always be welcomed by the aroma of fresh bread and an abundance of the best olive oil, cheese, olives and anchovies.

Graziella's salumeria (grocery store) on the main square of Adrano in the late '60's.

After studying in Milan, where he met my mother, my father soon became involved in the foundation of the organic movement in Sicily. This was in contrast to the industrial or 'conventional' agriculture based on the extensive use of chemicals that would soon sweep away centuries old traditions.

Since we were little, we were educated to taste the infinite variety of products available from the countryside surrounding Catania, our home town. Situated between Mount Etna and the beautiful Sicilian sea, we enjoyed sunny hot weather and fertile land. We were taught to recognise the seasonality on our plates, and we accompanied our parents on excursions to buy the best quality cheese, bread, oil and wine from local suppliers. While walking in the countryside, my parents would forage for berries and mushrooms, wild asparagus or whatever was in season. Our water came from a well near Etna as my parents chose not to use the water from the taps in Catania. They instead preferred the natural mineral water from a stream in the countryside. Once a week we would make the excursion to fetch our water, often on the way down from visiting friends on the side of Mount Etna.

There were other rituals we participated in that were linked to the transformation of food: like the three day process of making huge quantities of tomato sauce at my aunt Pina's house, an almost religious ritual that would guarantee the sauce for all the winter; the seasonal picking of grapes for winemaking (*vendemmia*), olive, orange and lemon picking in the scenic countryside near Noto in the extreme southern part of Sicily and the seasonal making of jams and pickles. On a daily basis, my mother's appreciation of the staples of Sicilian diet grew. She steadfastly devoted herself to learning to cook Italian food, how to prepare the many different kinds of beans, soups and the infinite varieties of pasta dishes. She had married into an Italian family and recognised the centrality of food in this culture that she had adopted. Knowing how to cook was almost obligatory!

My father was in charge of preparing the meat and fish dishes, often with the 'lesser' cuts of meat and innards and, most of all, with the fish bought by him at the fabulous Catania fish market and from the fishermen at the fishing port of Giarre. Here again, it was often the 'poor' fish like sardines and mackerel that he cooked and that experts today recognise, not only as the healthiest, but also the most sustainable to fish!

Since we were little we took part in the tradition of summer trips back and forth between Sicily and Ireland that Monica refers to and which became the topic of endless anecdotes and family stories. Like the one about my cousin Elayne who, as a toddler, having devoured a plate of spaghetti and, with her face literally covered in tomato sauce, innocently announced that she didn't like pasta sauce. That story has become legendary in our family! One summer it was my family who traveled back to Ireland, the next summer it was the Irish who came to Sicily. Most of the exchange, the bonding, the talking, the sharing and the lively discussions, happened around a table, often a shaky camping table.

Two cultures, and two families, got to know each other and learned to respect the differences and, in time, value and celebrate the many traits Ireland and Sicily have in common. I feel the depth of this intertwining as if I am a part of a great love story. And food has been one of, if not the, fundamental ingredient in this story.

Food's Central Place in Life

Growing up in this context and being a part of this story, I soon came to realise that looking for the ingredients, cooking and serving food are much more than their practical functions and carry a far greater symbolic meaning. For me, cooking is about taking care, showing love, creating harmony, warmth and bonding. It is also about keeping grounded when things get difficult, as they can sometimes in life. It is about exploring the senses, especially taste, smell, sight and touch but also being together as a family.

In my view it encapsulates all of our basic needs: material, emotional and social. We can experience our past, our memories, our traditions and rituals as families and communities. We celebrate our present, because we need to be fully in the present with our senses to enjoy the experience of exploring what we have on our plates and palates. We also invest in our future health and in the sustainability of life on the planet.

Food as an Act of Responsibility

Like my parents, I see food as an act of responsibility. We can make daily choices that have an impact on our health, on the health of the people we care about and on the health of the environment. We can choose to eat what is grown locally, that has been grown free of chemicals, to rely less on meat, eat more grains and unprocessed foods and to take time to cook and prepare food from scratch.

Italian cooking culture,in the broader context of the Mediterranean area, has historically been an ideal nutritional system and can still be considered so in many ways. The diet is rich in vegetables, fruit, wholegrains and olive oil with a moderate amount of fish, dairy and meat. These staples are complemented with condiments, spices and a glass of wine. Many studies associate this diet with longevity and even more importantly, wellness. In 2008, UNESCO proclaimed the Mediterranean diet to be a non-tangible heritage for humanity. They noted that this diet is not just about food; it's about ritual, customs, social interaction and building community. It is also respectful of the land, observes bio- diversity and ensures the conservation and development of local agriculture.

Italian cooking, or more generally the Mediterranean diet, is a grounded, nurturing way to ensure our health and to protect the planet from the dangers of climate changes. This diet enables us to safeguard the land, to honour the seasonality and the uniqueness of our local produce, to re-educate our senses to real food and to make quality agriculture a worthy economic and financial alternative. By making the right choices and enjoying our food every day with the people we care about, we can also fulfill our dream to create a more balanced economy and a better world to live in.

Maria Grazia Furnari

Main Square in Adrano where Maria Grazia's grandparents lived.

What is it about Italian cooking?

Quality of the Ingredients - local and seasonal

When Maria Grazia was preparing for the cookery classes in Dublin, what struck me first and foremost was the effort she put into sourcing good quality ingredients. These ingredients weren't necessarily expensive but she consistently wanted to ensure that the produce she bought was top quality. It seems that from there, miracles could happen.

When we went shopping together she preferred to shop in the local markets and to choose organic and local ingredients, where possible. When looking for mozzarella for the stuffed aubergines, she bypassed some of the cheaper versions of mozzarella, made from dried milk and was delighted to discover that we now produce lovely, fresh mozzarella in Ireland. When we went looking for tomatoes, she told me to "only buy them if they smell like tomatoes". Tomatoes really only taste great when in season.

We do not need to pay a whole lot more for food, but rather to make sure that it is "real" food. Ideally this is food that is in season,that has not traveled too far and that is organic or has not been contaminated with pesticides.

A Reverence for Food

When Paula travelled from Italy laden with wonderful Olive oil and Parmesan, she was, perhaps even unwittingly, fulfilling an important role in ensuring our lives were enriched.

She prized this oil and had travelled from Catania, where she lived, to a farm in a village on the side of Mount Etna to obtain it. She knew where to source good Parmesan cheese and the wine that accompanied their food was from the producer.

I have sat around a table with Italians listening to ongoing and detailed discussions about where to purchase good fish, good oil and so on. When they sit for a meal, they taste the food and then discuss it. Would it have been better if more salt had been added? Should it have been cooked for longer? Were the beans added too soon? This was not my experience of eating in Ireland and whilst things are changing and we value the pleasure of eating more now, we do not have the same culture of appreciation for food that they do in Mediterranean cultures.

A Willingness to Take Time

For soup, beans are soaked and cooked but the water is put to one side and used as stock when the soup is ready. When shellfish is cooked, the water is saved and becomes part of the sauce for the pasta. The water the broccoli is steamed in is used, if needed, when it is assembled with the pasta. Using cooking water really adds to the flavour of a dish. When making broccoli pasta, the cooked broccoli needs to be added to the garlic *before* being put in the pasta, to ensure that the broccoli absorbs some of the flavours before it meets the pasta. Maria Grazia was disappointed on one occasion that she had not allowed the broccoli more time with the garlic before she served the pasta dish. It is as if the ingredients all have their own personalities that need to be considered, known and taken advantage of to ensure that we get the best out of them!

Freshly bottled tomatoes for the winter

Fennel ready for picking

The Good Food Initiative

Towards A Healthy and Sustainable Food Culture

The Good Food Initiative was launched in early 2014 and the underlying philosophy is that we can underpin a healthy diet with recipes using ingredients that are of good quality, grown without chemicals and as much as possible are local and in season. We can take time to source and prepare wholesome, nourishing meals that are both simple and tasty. Furthermore, we believe that food is indeed healthier when prepared with care and love and enjoyed with others. It recognized that we can be bombarded with conflicting information on a daily basis about food and our health and this can be confusing!.

The key aspects of this initiative are to provide a forum where people can:

- Learn more about sourcing and preparing good food and to develop their own expertise and intuition about the role of food in maintaining good health.

- Be supported to take more responsibility for their health and recognize that the food we eat is a key ingredient in better health.

- Consider how we can source food in a way which is mindful of the impact on our environment and try to steer towards food that is local, in season and grown without chemicals.

- Recognise that the preparation and enjoyment of food can be nourishing and grounding in itself.

- Be involved in a community of like minded people who are striving to maintain their own health whilst ensuring the health of the environment.

Decisions around food are political. We make daily choices about where our food comes from. We can choose to eat unprocessed, local, seasonal produce and to re-educate our senses so as to appreciate food. We can choose to buy good food, eat less meat and buy what we can from Irish producers or even better grow it ourselves in our own gardens.

The Good Food Initiative has a regular blog on food, recipes and issues around food in Ireland. We also host regular classes on wholefood cooking and have also hosted classes in fermentation, bread making and incorporating seaweed into our diets. This publication is the second for the Good Food Initiative, the first being "The Secret to the Mince pies" a compilation of simple, wholesome recipes from the memories and hand written notes of Monica's late mother Christina Haughey.

The recipes that follow demonstrate how simple it can be to produce great food.

Good food is whole food, seasonal food, local food, food made with care and love

"Italian" Cooking

Different regional variations

While we talk about "Italian" food and understand that many of the ingredients and recipes have acquired national and international recognition, there is really no single, national Italian cooking tradition. Recipes and cooking practices vary according to regions, local climate and culture and consequent availability of different produce. Having grown up in Sicily, I was brought up with one of the most complex Italian cooking traditions, influenced by Greek, Arabic, Jewish, French and Spanish food culture. In my adult life I have been lucky to live both in Parma, in Emilia Romagna and also in Lucca in Tuscany and to learn always from real people around real tables. The cooking of Emilia Romagna is one of the 'richest' traditions, centred on meat, cream, stuffed ravioli, ragù, whilst Tuscan cookery is based on the 'poorest' ingredients, such as stale bread, grains and soups made from leftovers. I learned to experience how you can not only indulge in and celebrate "richness" and abundance, but also transform the simplest, 'poor' ingredients into wonderful meals and tastes to remember.

Graziella's daughter Lina (standing) having a picnic near Adrano on Mount Etna (c1965)

Olive tree

Contents

Soups

Only the pure of heart can make good soup

Beethoven

Minestrone

– "Zuppa"

When we think of soup we think of this one- it's popular all over Italy especially in winter. The more vegetables you add the better and the soup changes according to the seasons! In Tuscany Minestrone is known as Zuppa

Serves 4-6

Ingredients

- 2 onions
- 2 carrots
- A stalk of celery
- 4-5 leaves of black kale
- 100g of cabbage
- 2 courgettes
- 1 leek
- Any fresh vegetable in season (fennel, spinach, lettuce, peas, etc.)
- 1 large potato
- 2-3 fresh tomatoes or a cup of tomato passata
- *200 g fresh or cooked dried barlotti beans
- Fresh parsley or basil
- vegetable stock(approx 2 litres)
- black pepper
- parmesan cheese, to serve
- extra virgin olive oil
- fresh bread to serve

Method

Wash and dice all the vegetables.

Saute the onions, carrots and celery in a generous amount of olive oil for a few minutes. Then add the rest of the vegetables and the beans and cook for 10-15 minutes, stirring frequently. Add the tomatoes and enough stock to reach several cms over the vegetables. Bring to the boil, then lower the heat and leave to cook for approximately 1 1/2 hours during which time your kitchen will be filled with wonderfully appetising aromas.

Serve with extra virgin olive oil, black pepper, fresh basil or parsley and grated Parmesan cheese! You can also toast some tasty bread, such as Ciabatta and put it on the plate and cover with the minestrone.

*If using dried beans, soak overnight, drain and cook in a large saucepan of water until tender

Tuscan soup

– Farinata

*Kale is central in Tuscan cooking and this soup is a favourite in Lucca with locals.
Kale is grown all year round and is now of course grown in Ireland too.*

Serves 8-10

Ingredients

- 3 carrots
- 2 sticks celery
- 2 onions
- 10-15 black kale leaves
- 2-3 potatoes
- *500 g of fresh or cooked borlotti beans (dried)
- 300 g polenta (quick variety)
- ½ cup tomato passata
- Sage and garlic
- Salt and pepper
- Extra virgin olive oil

Method

Chop the onions, carrots, celery, kale and potatoes and put them
in a large pan with the oil. Sauté for 15 minutes.

When the beans are cooked, purée half the amount and add this
and the remaining whole cooked beans and all the cooking water
to the main pot with the vegetables.

Add passata and leave to cook for one hour.

Season with salt and pepper and add polenta to thicken.

Serve with oil and freshly ground pepper.

** If using dried beans they need to be soaked overnight. Then rinse
and put in a large saucepan and fill well with water. Add the sage
and garlic and cook until tender.*

Soaking the borlotti beans in cold water

Bread and tomato soup

"Pappa al pomodoro"

This is another popular soup in Tuscany. It's a 'poor' recipe because the ingredients are simple and cheap and you just need lots of fresh tomatoes and basil. You also need a loaf of 'good' bread, and ideally bread that is not fresh.

Serves 4-6

Ingredients

- 10-12 tablespoons of extra virgin olive oil
- 2 onions
- 4-5 cloves of garlic
- A large bunch of fresh basil
- 500-700 grams of bread roughly cut into cubes (the size of a thumb).
- *1 kg of peeled tomatoes
- Salt and pepper (black or chilli)
- (optional: the crust of parmesan)

Method

Gently heat half the olive oil in a large pot, add the chopped onions, garlic cloves (chopped) and half of the basil.

Add the bread and stir for 10 minutes until the bread fully absorbs the flavours.

Turn off the heat and leave to rest for half an hour. Add the tinned tomatoes and half a litre of vegetable stock.

Season with salt, pepper and add the remaining basil.

(Some people add the crust of the Parmesan to add taste!)

Leave to cool a bit and before serving add the remaining olive oil and a few basil leaves for each serving.

*(If fresh tomatoes not available use a good quality tinned version. With fresh tomatoes put them into boiling water for 5 minutes and then peel them under cold water)

Primi

Pesto

It transforms any pasta into a delicious meal

The traditional recipe is the one from Liguria made with fresh basil, garlic, oil, pinenuts and parmesan cheese. There are many other different kinds of pesto and the key is to have an oily nut (pine nut, almond, hazelnut etc), extra virgin olive oil, some parmesan cheese, garlic and a herb such as basil or a vegetable such as pepper, courgette, aubergine or kale can be used.

In Sicily we use local ingredients like almonds, capers, olives or sundried tomatoes to add flavour and give character to the more gentle northern pesto.

Pesto experts argue that without garlic it cannot be called pesto

Basil and mint can give pesto its freshness and lightness

These recipes demonstrate how easy it is to make your own pesto and are an introduction to some of the many possibilities.

Pasta with black kale pesto

- Pasta al pesto di cavolo nero

Since my daughter Carolina ate this in an up-market restaurant in Florence we have been re creating it at home. This is our version and it is really tasty.

Serves 4 people

Ingredients

- 10 -12 leaves of black kale,
- 50g almonds
- 1 clove garlic,
- 4-5 tablespoons of extra virgin olive oil
- 100g grated parmesan plus parmesan to serve (1-2 tablespoons for person)
- 500 g pasta,
- Black pepper

Method

Chop the kale roughly and either steam or boil in salted water for about 10 mins until tender.

Drain and put in a blender with the almonds, garlic and oil and blend until smooth and creamy.

To finish stir in the grated parmesan.

Fry the bacon with oil until crunchy

Cook the pasta in salted water, drain, add the pesto, the bacon, more parmesan and serve hot.

Note: If the pesto seems thick then add a little water from the pasta

Variation: Add 150 g smoked bacon or speck to make the pesto really flavoursome

Pasta with aubergine pesto

- Pasta al pesto di melanzane

In Sicily aubergines are so plentiful that there at least 50 recipes with aubergines. They work well in a pesto as it has a smooth texture. Cooking them in oil on a pan is tasty but they absorb a lot of oil. The healthier option is to grill or bake, with a light coating of oil, if you like. They can actually be cooked without oil.

Serves 4

Ingredients

- 2 - 3 aubergines
- 1 or 2 cloves of garlic
- A bunch of fresh basil
- 50 g of dried almonds (unpeeled)
- 100 g grated parmesan
- 500 g pasta
- Fresh mint
- Extra virgin olive oil

Method

Peel the aubergines and slice thinly.

Grill the aubergines or fry in a large pan with the oil for approximately 15 minutes or until brown.

To make the pesto, using a blender, mix together the garlic, almonds, aubergine and basil. When smooth stir in the grated parmesan.

Bring pasta water to the boil, add salt and the pasta and cook until ready.

Drain and add the pesto.

Top with fresh basil and mint leaves.

"Ho buttato la pasta!"

The pasta is on!

Some of the basics about pasta

What kind?

Many of these recipes contain pasta. As unrefined flour is always best, it is good to choose wholemeal wheat or spelt pasta, or gluten-free if you have a sensitivity to wheat. As a compromise for my children, I often mix wholemeal with white pasta. If you can, choose organic pasta as grains, especially wheat, are often adulterated with chemicals. There is a lot of poor quality pasta and I believe it is important to seek out good quality varieties, preferably organic or made by a small producer. Sometimes people who are sensitive to wheat can tolerate organic wheat or spelt.

Pasta has a huge significance in Italian cooking culture and there are hundreds of recipes with pasta and the different regions have developed their own shape, texture and size. And of course, Italians have views on which shape best matches which sauce. I have not addressed this in the recipes except to say that penne pasta is quite versatile and matches many of the sauces. Fresh pasta is usually made by hand or with simple pasta making machines but it is essentially a mix of eggs and flour and often given a filling.

How to Cook Pasta !

Like most people in Ireland, I generally use dried pasta as it is possible to get good quality pasta and, obviously, it is more convenient for every day cooking. It is important to check the timing on the packet as each type requires a different cooking time. At home we boil up a big pan of cold water although I know many people boil a kettle. Either way is fine, but the pasta needs plenty of water and when the water comes to the boil, salt it and add the pasta. Cook it with the lid off and occasionally stir it to ensure the pasta does not stick. This is particularly important with spaghetti and with fresh pasta.

Once the pasta is on we normally announce to everyone at home "Ho Buttato la pasta" as it is important that diners are alert to the fact that in less than ten minutes the pasta will be ready and can't wait. Pasta is best eaten right away unless it is for a salad. I have also heard my extended Irish family announce that "The pasta is on", meaning get ready for the meal. To check that it is cooked, you can take a strand and eat it. In Italy it is eaten "al dente" where there is still a "bite" to it and Italians say it is more digestible slightly under cooked. It is best to develop the habit of keeping some pasta water in case the sauce needs more liquid or needs thickening. I often drain the pasta early and finish the cooking on the pan, adding pasta water as is needed. Many Italians, including myself, believe that extra virgin olive oil is the best oil to use in cooking. There is much research about the need to be careful when cooking with oils. The heat should be kept low, ensuring the olive oil does not burn and thus becoming potentially harmful to our health. In Italian cooking, parmesan is used liberally and often the oil is added at the end, a delicious and healthy way to use the oil.

A Family wedding in Sicily in the 1960's

Graziella (front left hand side) and her daughters Lina (next to her mother) and Lucia (opposite) and cousin Salvatore (next to Lucia) with Aldo and other family members.

Sicilian style pasta

- Pasta con i broccoli arriminati

This is a very simple and tasty pasta.

Serves 4

Ingredients

- 4 - 5 broccoli spears
- 3 - 4 garlic cloves (chopped small)
- 6 - 8 cherry tomatoes or 1/2 cup tomato passata
- 500 g pasta
- Extra virgin olive oil (half a cup)
- 1 teaspoon chilli powder
- Grated parmesan cheese to serve

Method

Bring to boil a pot of salted water.

Wash and cut the broccoli into small pieces and put in the salted water.
Cook for 5-7 minutes and remove from the water when almost cooked and put aside.
Keep the pot of broccoli water.

In a large frying pan put the garlic, the oil and fry for a few minutes.

Chop the tomatoes and add to the pan. Put the lid on and cook for a few minutes.

Add the pasta to the pot of broccoli water and cook for required time.

Meanwhile add the cooked broccoli to the frying pan and mash
and cook gently with the garlic to make a sauce.

When the pasta is ready keep aside a cup of pasta water and drain.

Add the cooked pasta to the pan and stir well until it soaks in all of the flavours.
Add some of the saved cooking water if dry.

Serve with chilli and parmesan.

Statue of Vincenzo Bellini in Catania, Sicily

Bellini was famous for the opera Norma.

Catanese pasta

- Pasta alla Norma

This pasta takes its name from a famous opera composer, Vincenzo Bellini, who was born in Catania. The legend is that when people first tasted this pasta they felt it was so magnificent that it should be given the name of Bellini's most famous opera, Norma. Ricotta cheese is fabulous with aubergines and is now being made in Ireland.

Serves 4 - 5

Ingredients

- 2 large or 3 small aubergines
- 2 garlic cloves
- 1 bottle of tomato passata (750 g)
- 150 g salted dried ricotta (or fresh ricotta if available)
- 500 g small shaped pasta (*penne, fusilli*, etc.)

Method

Cut aubergines in slices and grill or fry in olive oil.
They are ready when they turn brown.
Put these aside and keep warm until serving.

Peel the garlic and put in a pan with a few spoonfuls of oil.
Add the passata and the fresh basil and cook for 10-15 minutes.
You can take the garlic out when ready.

Put on the pasta water to boil and when boiling add salt and the pasta and cook.

When the pasta is ready, drain and mix in the tomato sauce
and serve with grated ricotta, two or three slices of aubergine for each plate
and top with fresh basil.

Ravioli alla Norma

In Parma, I learnt how to make ravioli and adapted the traditional Sicilian recipe. It is slightly more complicated than the Sicilian Norma but easier than it looks. It would help to have a ravioli "cutter" which are quite inexpensive. If you do not have one, just use a small pastry cutter.

Serves 4-5

Ingredients

- 50 g white pasta flour
- 4 eggs
- 3 aubergines
- 2/3 cloves of garlic
- 250 g fresh ricotta cheese
- 300 g cherry tomatoes
- 250 g dried ricotta cheese
- A pinch of salt
- Extra virgin olive oil
- Fresh basil

Method

To make the filling
Peel aubergines with a knife and put the skins aside.
Slice the aubergines thinly and grill or cube them and fry gently in a pan for 10-15 minutes with some oil and 1 clove of garlic. When cooked put in a bowl and mash with a fork to make a puree.
Add the fresh ricotta cheese and leave to cool.

To make the pasta
Put flour on a board or table, make a hole in the centre, add eggs, oil and start mixing gently with a fork. Work with hands for 15 minutes approx. until it becomes elastic.
When you push your finger into the dough, the indentation should flatten quickly.
Cut the dough into slices 2 cm thick and roll each out with a rolling pin until the dough becomes thin.
Put a teaspoonful of mixture at a distance of 5 cm one from the other.
Cover the ravioli with a layer of pasta and then cut the pasta using the ravioli cutter.
Cook in boiling water and when they come to surface keep cooking for 2-3 minutes until tender.

To assemble
In a large pan cook cherry tomatoes with garlic and basil for 5 minutes.
Cut the aubergines skins into very thin slices and fry until crispy.
Put some tomato sauce on a plate, add 3 - 4 ravioli and sprinkle with grated dried ricotta, a few fried aubergines skins and some fresh basil. Serve.

1.

2.

3.

4.

Risotto with courgettes, smoked bacon and cheese

- Risotto affumicato alle zucchine

My daughter Michela loves risotto and had the idea that the risotto with courgettes would be even tastier with bacon and cheese and it is!

Serves 4-5

Ingredients

- 500 g risotto rice (*carnaroli*)
- 2 onions
- 1 litre (approx) vegetable stock
- ½ glass white wine
- A knob of butter
- 200 g of grated parmesan cheese
- 300 g courgettes
- A slice of thick speck (smoked bacon)
- 100 g smoked Cheese

Method

Chop finely the onions, the courgettes and speck. Put in a large pan with oil and let cook for 10 minutes.

Add rice and cook for 5 more minutes.

Add the wine and cook for 5 minutes.

Prepare some vegetable stock and when boiling, add a small amount every few minutes for a total of 15 minutes.
The rice like the pasta has to be '*al dente.*'

Add the butter, parmesan and smoked cheese.

Pasta with courgettes

- *Pasta ca cucuzza*

I have fond memories of my cousin Lina making this for me in her house in Catania. it is a simple pasta but delicious, as the basil really brings out the best in the courgettes!

Serves 4-5

Ingredients

- 4 courgettes (medium sized)
- Extra virgin olive oil
- Fresh basil
- Black pepper
- Pasta (500 g) of the prefered shape (ideally *pennette* or *spaghetti*)
- 1-2 cloves of garlic
- Grated parmesan
- Salt

Method

Cut the courgettes into long thin slices. Fry gently in the oil with the garlic. When fried, set aside and add the fresh basil.

Bring water to boil, add salt, add the pasta and cook for required time.

Drain the pasta and mix with the courgettes.

Add freshly ground black pepper and parmesan cheese.

Capers in salt

Pasta with capers and olives

- Pasta agli odori di Sicilia

This simple Sicilian pasta recipe involves very little cooking but incorporates some strong flavours from that region and is a great quick dish.

Serves 4 - 5

Ingredients

- 2 tbsp capers (if in salt, soak in warm water for 15 minutes)
- 2-3 cloves of garlic
- 2-3 anchovies
- 50 g black olives
- 10 cherry tomatoes (chopped)
- 500 g pasta (*spaghetti* or *fusilli* shape)
- 100 g grated parmesan
- Extra virgin olive oil
- Sea salt and chilli powder

Method

Take a large frying pan and add a generous amount of oil.

Add the capers, chopped garlic, anchovies and olives
and cook together for 5 minutes.

Crush the mixture with a fork until it becomes a paste.

Add the chopped tomatoes and cook for a further 5 minutes.

Boil the pasta water, add salt and cook pasta for required time.

Drain the pasta and add the anchovy paste to the pan and mix well.

Add the chilli powder and serve hot with the grated parmesan.

Gnocchi di patate

A typical first course in many regions, gnocchi can be made with different types of flours or vegetables but potato gnocchi are nowadays the most popular

Serves 4

Ingredients

- 1 kg "floury" potatoes
- 1 egg
- A pinch of salt
- 250 g plain flour (approx-the quantity of flour depends on the potatoes)

(some people peel the potatoes but I prefer to leave the skins on as it's healthier-but as you prefer)

Method

Boil the potatoes and drain and mash well.

Put the mashed potato on a floured surface and add the egg, the salt and half the quantity of the flour and mix with your hands.

Keep adding the flour until the mixture is soft, elastic but not sticky.

Divide the dough into approx ten parts and roll out each until it resembles a snake with your little finger as diameter. Cut into 1-2 cm gnocchi.

Sprinkle with flour so the gnocchi don't stick to each other

Boil water with salt in a big and wide pan, add the gnocchi.

The gnocchi is cooked when they rise to the surface, this only takes a few minutes.

Remove the gnocchi gently with a perforated spoon.

Serve with favourite sauce.

I love to serve gnocchi simply with basil pesto or tomato sauce, fresh basil and mozzarella cheese. My family loves them with melted gorgonzola cheese, bacon and parmesan. Butter or extra virgin olive oil and parmesan are also a good and quick way of serving gnocchi and enjoy their flavour

Sides

Tomatoes au gratin

- Pomodori gratinati

Makes 10 servings

Ingredients

- 5 tomatoes
- 2 slices crusty bread
- 1 garlic clove
- Basil
- 100 g parmesan
- Extra virgin olive oil

Method

Preheat oven to 180°C or gas mark 4

Cut the tomatoes in half and take out the seeds.

Cut the bread into small pieces, add the crushed garlic, basil,
parmesan and enough oil to bind the ingredients.
(This can be done with food processor if you wish)

Fill the tomatoes with the mixture, coat in oil and bake for 15-20 minutes.

Fennel au gratin

- *Finocchi gratinati*

Serves 4

Ingredients

- 2-3 fennel bulbs
- 1 bay leaf
- 50 g grated parmesan
- 50 g other "tasty" cheese, e.g. smoked (diced)
- Extra virgin olive oil
- 50g breadcrumbs

Method

Pre-heat oven to 180^0C or gas 4.

Wash and cut the fennel in halves and then into slices and steam for 5-10 minutes.

Grease an oven dish with olive oil, put in the fennel and cover with the cheese, parmesan, bay leaf in pieces and the breadcrumbs.

Season with salt, pepper and olive oil and put in oven until the breadcrumbs become crispy and light brown.

Serve warm.

Cauliflower balls

- 'Polpette'

This is a lovely comfort food and children really love them. These are my invention and a great way to get children to eat cauliflower.

Makes 10-15 servings

Ingredients

- 1 cauliflower
- 2-3 potatoes
- 1 egg
- 100 g of grated parmesan
- Salt
- Black pepper
- Extra virgin olive oil
- 50 g breadcrumbs

Method

Preheat oven to 180°C or gas mark 4.

Cut the cauliflower and potatoes in cubes and steam until tender.
Put in a large bowl and with a fork reduce to a puree.
Leave to cool for a few minutes.

Add the egg, parmesan, salt and pepper.

Make the mixture into little balls (*polpette*) with your hands
and cover in breadcrumbs.

Grease a large baking tin, and put the *polpette* into the tin
and add a little drizzle of oil to each.

Cook in oven for 15-20 minutes or until crispy.

A favourite Sicilian contorno

- Caponata

A favourite Sicilian side dish that is luscious and is a favourite in my family. It is a summer dish and some families store it in jars for the winter when these vegetables are out of season. It has an Arabic influence with a sweet and sour element.

Serves 4

Ingredients

- 2-3 aubergines
- 2-3 peppers
- 3 sticks celery
- 1 onion
- 3 dessert spoons capers
- 3-4 tbsp olives
- Fresh basil and mint
- 1/2 cup passata
- 10 toasted almonds
- Red wine vinegar
- Salt and pepper
- Extra virgin olive oil

Method

Slice the celery thinly and boil gently for 10 minutes.

Meanwhile, finely dice the aubergines, peppers and onions.

Fry the aubergines gently for 10 minutes in a large frying pan with oil and put aside.

Then fry the peppers separately and when almost done add the onions.

Cook gently for a few more minutes to allow the flavours to combine.

Combine all the cooked vegetables on the pan and add the passata, olives and capers.

Season with salt, pepper and vinegar.

Sweeten with a spoon of sugar if desired.

Before serving add in fresh basil, mint and toasted almonds.

Serve hot or cold.

Aubergine bake

- *Parmigiana*

Traditionally this is made with fried aubergines but I prefer using grilled aubergines as it is lighter. There are regional varieties of this dish and in Sicily they add ham and hard boiled eggs.

Serves 4

Ingredients

- 2-3 big or 4-5 small aubergines
- 1 bottle of tomato passata
- 2 garlic cloves
- 100 g grated parmesan
- 250 g fresh mozzarella cheese
- Large bunch of fresh basil
- Salt
- Extra virgin olive oil

Method

Pre-heat the oven to 180°C or gas mark 4.

Wash the aubergines, cut into thin slices and grill until cooked.

Dice the mozzarella into small pieces and leave to drain for 15 minutes.

In the meantime make the tomato sauce by putting the oil, crushed garlic, a few leaves of basil and the passata in a pan and gently cook for 10 minutes. Season when ready.

Put some oil on a baking tin, add a layer of aubergines, and then a thin layer of mozzarella, fresh basil and parmesan and cover with the passata. Continue to alternate the layers of aubergines, mozzarella, basil, parmesan and passata.

Cover finally with remaining passata and put in the oven for 20-25 minutes.

You can serve hot or cold.

Broccoli pie

- *Scacciata*

This is a Sicilian dish that is popular at Christmas time if having friends over. Here I use broccoli but cauliflower will also suffice and sausages can be added. It is similar to focaccia but has a filling.

Serves 6

Ingredients

- 500 g flour
- 25 g dried yeast
- 5 teaspoons extra virgin olive oil
- Pinch of salt
- 300 g broccoli (washed and cut into small pieces with hard parts removed)
- 50 g black olives
- 100 g smoked or other tasty cheese
- 3-5 spring onions
- Salt
- Chilli powder
- Extra virgin olive oil

Method

Preheat oven to 200°C or gas mark 6.

To make the dough, mix the yeast with half a cup warm water.

Mix the flour with the olive oil, add the yeast mixture and salt and knead until smooth (15 minutes).

Cover with a damp cloth and put in a warm place for 1 hour (approximately) until it doubles in size.

Divide the dough in half and roll the first part (50 mm thick) and place on a large greased baking tray.

Add the broccoli, grated cheese, olives, chopped onions and plenty of olive oil.

Roll out the remainder of the dough and use this to cover the pie.

Seal the sides of the *scacciata* with your fingers to prevent the stuffing from coming out.

Sprinkle the top with a spoonful of oil and spread with your hands. Make holes with a fork and put in the hot oven for approximately 20 minutes.

Serve warm or at room temperature.

Pumpkin and mushroom gateau

- Sformato di zucca e funghi

Gateau with potato or other vegetables is very popular all over Italy and it transforms vegetables into a really tasty meal. My version uses a pumpkin which is very common in autumn and very tasty.

Serves 4 - 6

Ingredients

- 500 g pumpkin
- 1-2 potatoes
- 200 g mushrooms
- 2 garlic cloves
- 1 egg
- Nutmeg
- Smoked cheese
- Fresh parsley
- Black pepper
- 100 g parmesan
- 3 tbsp breadcrumbs

Method

Preheat oven to 200⁰C or gas mark 6.

Boil the potatoes and peel them.

Peel the pumpkin and cut into big pieces, put in baking tray and cook in the oven until soft (approximately 15 minutes). Fry some garlic in a little olive oil for a few minutes and then add the sliced mushrooms and the parsley and cook for a further 5 minutes until mushrooms are nicely browned.

Mash the pumpkin and the potatoes with a fork, add the egg, salt, black pepper, nutmeg and parmesan.

Grease a deep baking tray and put half of the potato mixture and cover with the mushrooms, cheese and then the rest of the mixture.
Sprinkle with breadcrumbs and oil.

Bake in oven for approximately 20 minutes or until brown.

Lino Olivieri's Olive Oil

Lino Olivieri has been bringing olive oil from his family farm in Puglia to Ireland since 1999.

Like Paula Eagar he too treasures this wonderful oil and believes Irish people should be able to enjoy its benefits. His oil has a unique rich fruity aroma that captures the essence of the nearby wild herbs such as wild fennel and rosemary.

The oil is cold pressed using stone mills and grown without fertilizers.

For more info and how to purchase this wonderful high quality product see:

www.olivierioliveoil.com

Lino Olivieri's apple cake (with extra virgin olive oil)

Ingredients

- 5 medium sized apples
- 1 lemon
- 50g raisins (rinsed)
- 50g pine nuts
- 5 free range eggs
- 200g caster sugar
- 300g self raising flour
- 200 g Olivieri Extra Virgin Olive oil
- 5g sea salt
- 1 teaspoon of ground cinnamon

Method

Pre heat the oven to 180⁰C gas mark 4

Grease a medium sized "Ring cake tin" (round cake tin with hole in the centre)

Peel the apples and slice thinly and mix them in a large bowl with the juice of the lemon, raisins and pine nuts and ground cinnamon.

In another bowl combine the eggs, sugar, olive oil and sea salt and mix well with a wooden spoon or hand-mixer.

Fold in the flour and add the apple with raisin and pine nuts.

Pour the mixture into the prepared tin and cover with tin foil.

Bake the cake for 30 minutes.

After this time take off the tin foil and bake for a further 15-20 minutes.

Leave to sit for 10 minutes and then remove gently from tin and dust with icing sugar.

The cake will keep for 4-5 days –if it will last!

Variations: You can use other nuts such a cashews or hazel nuts- just chop them a little before adding

Organic Irish Growers

Nurney Farm

In 1990, Deirdre O'Sullivan and Norman Kenny invested in 14 acres of land and a derelict farmhouse in Kildare. Today, they farm 40 acres of land, run an organic vegetable shop from their base in Carbury, and grow a large range of organic fruit and vegetables for farmer's markets in Trim, The Green Door (Dublin 8) as well as supplying Irish wholesalers.

Among the many vegetables they grow are courgettes, brocolli, peas, aubergines and tomatoes, all very suitable for pasta sauces!

www.organicveg.ie

Norman Kenny and Deirdre O'Sullivan of Nurney Farm

For further information on Irish organic growers see

www.iofga.org